ENRICO ROLLA

52 thoughts

to guide your life

Text: Enrico Rolla (www.iwatson.com; www.iwatsoneducation.com)
Layout: Cristina Cecconato - acapoagency (TO)
Illustrations: Barnaba Orrù

Published by Istituto Watson Edizioni
C.so Vinzaglio 12/bis (TO)
Tel. 0115611102 fax 0115611102
e-mail: info@iwatson.com- progetti@iwatson.com
www.iwatson.com
www.iwatsoneducation.com

Printed by:

CreateSpace
CreateSpeace Indipendent Publishing Platform
www.createspace.com

First Edition: 2009 Torino
© by Istituto Watson
Second Edition: 2012 Torino (10 Ristampe al 2016)
© by SEI-Società Editrice Internazionale
Third Edition: 2016
© Istituto Watson Edizioni
C.so Vinzaglio 12/bis, Torino
10121

52 thoughts to guide your life

This book is intended to help people who want to "spice up" their lives. It is a proverbial "kick up the backside". All you have to do is ponder carefully each thought and if you think it applies to you, act upon it. You will soon start feeling uplifted, self-confident and fulfilled.

Everything we tell ourselves can shape our life, what we tell can lead us in one direction or another, to promote, or even hinder our own life projects, to work against us leaving a feeling of frustration or anger. We may even end up depressed or with precipitating self-esteem. Our thoughts can be friends or enemies and it is up to us to find a way to move in a more positive direction. It should be our life aim to feel good and to take care of ourselves. **It is only through positivity that we can reach a true sense of well-being.**

Let's start with the Milwaukee YMCA motto:

Pay attention to your thoughts, they will become your words.
Pay attention to your words, they will become your deeds,
Pay attention to your deeds, they will become your habits,
Pay attention to your habits, they will become your character,
Pay attention to your character, it will become your destiny.

1

If you find yourself distressed or uneasy and you say **"This is me, it's the way I am. There's nothing I can do about it"**. Things will only get worse. Over time, it easier to "rot" rather than "ripen."

2

Compete with yourself. **Competing with others doesn't make you any stronger.** You risk relying on other people's opinion.

3

Always face anxiety.
Every time you manage to overcome your distress you will gradually become freer.
Don't let anxiety decide matters for you.

4

It's too easy to point out other people's mistakes. **Don't ever be frugal with praise and appreciation**, it helps others improve.
The more you compare yourself to others, **the weaker you will become.**
Do not depend on other people's opinion.

5

The more you see others as important or unimportant, **the more you make yourself weak.** You will find yourself dependent on the opinions of others.

6

It is not always easy to find people to learn from. Take the opportunity whenever you can.

7

Don't focus on other people's defects. It will only encourage your own frustration and anger. It is not the way to peacefulness.

8

Reducing anxiety is up to you. Don't delegate the job to drugs, alcohol or food.

9

Be detached when observing your negative thoughts. Don't let them become your reality. They are only thoughts.

10

Don't tell yourself "my bad mood will pass".
You must make it pass.

11

Don't make other peoples' problems become your own. If you do, you will suffer with them, not help them.

12

Don't say "I can do this better than you."
**Keep your thoughts to yourself and avoid
making comparisons.**

13

Don't be afraid to give.
You will be afraid only if your wish is to take.
Giving will be returned to you.
You can only take once.

14

Often we help others **to help ourselves and not always for their benefit.**

15

For each daily activity, just put in the right amount of effort and no more. **Going into a fit won't improve your performance**, it just muddies the waters.

16

One up-manship doesn't work - **you'll fall at the first hurdle.**

17

If some want to see you up on a pedestal, go for it. But be prepared to fall when others start sawing down the base.

18

Conceitedness and arrogance with whoever you consider inferior is not the way forward. **You risk taking yourself far too seriously.**

19

No one person is more important than another.
There are only those who are more or less
congenial.

20

Don't presume that others will recognize your needs. State them plainly. But accept that your needs may not be the same as theirs.

21

Your sense of well-being depends on you alone and not on outside factors.
It's easy to feel goodwhen everything is going well at work and athome. Everyone can do this. If you tell yourself "Feeling good or bad depends on what's going on out there", you'll never be able to focus on yourself to make the necessary changes.

22

Remember that words are not deeds.
It's very easy to make promises. If you believe
in deceitful promises, you'll get angry at your
falsehearted friends rather than with yourself
for having taken the bait.

23

Asking yourself "Where did I go wrong?"
brings only advantages

24

Don't undermine or put others down.
They will only learn dependency and not how
to be your ally.

25

Not liking the way something is done,
thinking "I would have done it differently",
will make you even more intolerant.
This behaviour fuels your own need to
be aggressive.

26

Never say: "I've always been here for you."
Don't do "favours" that are sacrifices
designed to make you feel that somebody owes
you something.

27

**Don't expect people to be different to what
they appear to be.**
You can't change them. You will end up feeling
unfulfilled trying to do so.

28

Giving advice is easy and anyone can do it.
Better to remain silent, unless you are able to
convey something useful.

29

Accept criticism.
Don't let it bother you - and take from it
what is useful.

30

Don't impose your wishes on others. Observe theirs and take account of your own and **look for a compromise between yours and theirs.**

31

Expectations like "It is bound to go well!" are useless. **Be committed to reach your objective. But take nothing for granted.** If your expectations do not transpire, you risk disappointment and hurt, wasting too much time for recovery.

32

Envy is not the way to improvement,
it just makes you feel bad.

33

Ask yourself if the criticism you serve out is designed to demonstrate that you are the better. **If that is so, you are surely weaker than those you criticise.**

34

Being glad for other people's success helps to create friends and be happy.

35

Getting angry costs effort and every time creates a small loss. Sure, by getting angry you can dominate others. **But in doing so you risk creating an emptiness around you.**

36

Make rules for yourself and be sure to respect them. Don't make excuses when you can't. **You are only taking yourself for a ride.**

37

Laugh at yourself, not at others.

38

Commitment to success or to acquire prestige is worthy. But in doing so, watch from above and **laugh at yourself while observing.**

39

Allow for a few vices.
But don't let them become your master.

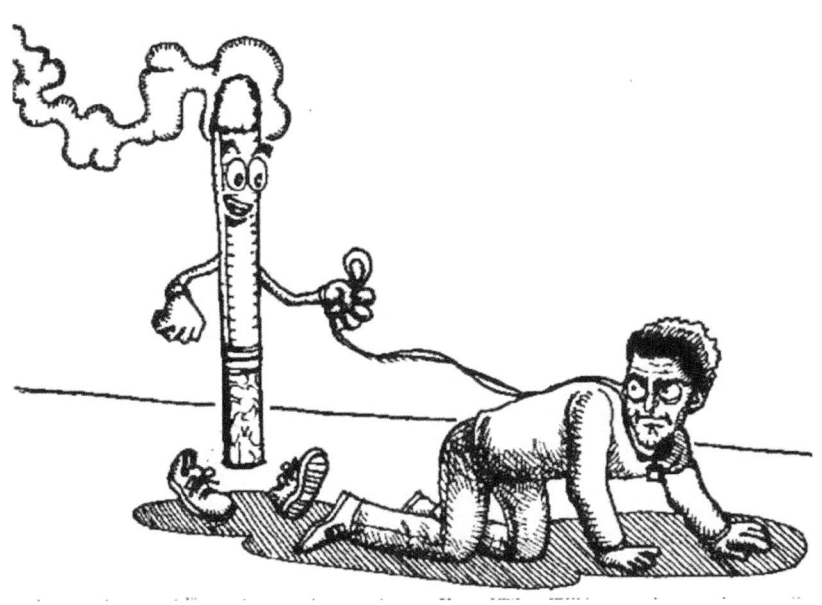

40

Your first duty is towards yourself. **If you are gratified, those around you will benefit.**

41

Your relatives or friends, more than anyone else, have the power to make you suffer. But just think: "That's the way they are, I can't change them, I can only try to understand why." **Let their words slide like water off a duck's back.**

42

Love is accepting others as they are and not wanting to change them.

43

Telling yourself: "I would be happy if I could manage to find the right partner", **risks, in the future, creating not only your own unhappiness but also theirs.**

44

To love is finding contentment in another's happiness. If a person says: "I'm going away to look for new experiences" you will be ready to understand and accept.
If you feel profound distress it is because you depend on your partner.
To love is not dependency or need of another.

45

Don't allow the needs of others to come before your own. You'll end up suffering and blame your suffering on the other person.

46

If you want to help someone, don't feel that
you have to satisfy their needs.
Teach them to satisfy their own.

47

Avoid complaining: it annoys others and nothing useful comes out of it.

48

If you want to help someone, **don't let them lean on you.** They might end up falling down and get hurt.

49

Don't lean on others.
If they move, you'll fall.

50

If you need love, don't reach with outstretched arms, holding love in your hands and relegating the weight of your happiness to another.

51

When designing your future don't say: "I would like to, I could, I should ...."
Only **"I will do it "** can become your future.

52

Can we really practice what we preach?
**Perhaps, every now and again we should put
ourselves to the test.**

The Watson Institute, under the direction of **Enrico Rolla**, is a research, training and consulting society since 1979. It operates in the field of applied psychology and it is the Regional center of A.I.A.M.C., (Italian Association of Analysis and Modification of Behaviour) part of European Association for Behavioural and Cognitive Therapies (EABCT).

COGNITIVE BEHAVIOUR THERAPY

The Institute has over 35 years' **experience in evidence-based treatment for several disorders**. Following international guidelines from the National Institute for Care and Excellence (UK) and the National Institute of Mental health (USA) we provide CBT sessions, all-day intensive training, online therapy for panic attacks, obsessive compulsive disorder, phobias, social anxiety, depression, eating disorders, gambling and personality disorders.

SCHOOL FOR SPECIALIZATION IN COGNITIVE BEHAVIOUR THERAPY

The Watson Institute is a post degree school of behavioural and cognitive psychotherapy for physicians and psychologists recognised by the *Ministero dell'Università e della Ricerca Scientifica e Tecnologica* (G.U. n 92 del 21/01/98 - *Official Gazette of the Italian Republic)*

ORGANIZATION BEHAVIOUR MODIFICATION

We provide business seminars, workshops and vocational training in communication, sales techniques, human resources management, career empowerment, marketing & organization.

Contacts:

Istituto Watson - Torino
C.so Vinzaglio 12/bis – Tel/Fax 011 5611102

Istituto Watson - Chivasso
c/o "il Campus" via Baraggino – Tel/Fax 011 5611102

E-mail: *info@iwatson.com – progetti@iwatson.com*
Sites: *www.iwatson.com – www.iwatsoneducation.com*

www.ingramcontent.com/pod-product-compliance
Lightning Source LLC
Chambersburg PA
CBHW060337290526
45793CB00003B/645